NOMPILO NXUMALO

# YouTube Shorts Exposed: The Hidden Formula for Instant Virality

*How Top Creators Get Millions of Views—And How You Can Too!*

# Contents

# 1

# Introduction

The internet has changed the way we consume content, and YouTube Shorts is at the forefront of this revolution. In just a few seconds, a well-crafted short-form video can capture millions of eyeballs, spreading like wildfire across the platform. The potential is undeniable—creators with zero subscribers have skyrocketed to fame overnight, and businesses have leveraged Shorts to build powerful brands with nothing more than a smartphone. Yet, while many dream of virality, only a handful ever achieve it. Why? Because success on YouTube Shorts isn't about luck—it's about understanding the game.

Most people believe that viral content is a matter of chance, that some creators get "lucky" while others remain unnoticed. But that couldn't be further from the truth. If luck were the driving force, how do certain creators consistently rack up millions of views, time and time again? The reality is simple: there is a hidden formula—a set of strategies that work every single time, allowing those who master them to break through the algorithm and dominate YouTube Shorts effortlessly.

This book is your backstage pass to the world of viral Shorts. No more guessing. No more hoping for a lucky break. You're about to unlock the exact blueprint used by top creators—strategies that have been tested, proven, and repeated to generate millions of views. Every technique, every secret, and every mistake to avoid has been broken down in a way that is easy to understand and apply. Whether you're starting from scratch or looking to scale your content to the next level, the insights in this book will give you a clear, actionable path to success.

By the time you turn the last page, you won't just understand why some videos explode in popularity while others fade into obscurity—you'll have the tools to make your own Shorts go viral. The question is, are you ready to step into the spotlight?

# 2

# Chapter 1: Cracking the YouTube Shorts Algorithm

The secret behind viral YouTube Shorts lies in the invisible force that controls everything: the algorithm. Contrary to popular belief, YouTube doesn't randomly decide which videos to push to millions and which to bury in obscurity. There's a precise science behind it, a system designed to reward content that captivates and retains viewers. The algorithm's one true goal is simple—keep people watching. The longer users stay on the platform, the more ads they see, and the more money YouTube makes. This means that Shorts capable of hooking viewers from the very first second and holding their attention are given priority, pushed to massive audiences, and set on the path to virality.

But what exactly makes a Short worthy of promotion? The answer lies in two critical metrics: engagement and retention. Engagement measures how much viewers interact with your video—likes, comments, shares, and rewatches all send powerful signals to YouTube that your content is valuable. The more people engage, the more the algorithm pushes your Short to new audiences. However, engagement alone isn't enough. Retention—how long viewers actually watch your video—plays an even bigger role. If people drop off within the first few seconds, the algorithm sees your video as uninteresting and stops promoting it. But if viewers stay hooked until the very last second, or even rewatch it, YouTube takes that as a sign of high-quality content and pushes it further, multiplying your reach exponentially.

Understanding these key metrics is what separates struggling creators from those who dominate the platform. It's not about luck, chance, or even the size of your channel—it's about mastering the art of engagement and retention. Once you crack this code, you can make the algorithm work for you, turning every Short into a potential viral hit.

YouTube isn't just a video-sharing platform—it's a business, and like any business, its success depends on keeping customers engaged. The longer people stay on YouTube, the more ads they watch, and the more money the platform makes. That's why YouTube Shorts isn't just about entertaining clips—it's a strategic tool designed to capture attention, retain viewers, and keep them scrolling. If your content aligns with this goal, YouTube will reward you generously, pushing your videos to wider audiences and multiplying your chances of virality.

To do this, YouTube prioritizes content that keeps viewers hooked from start to finish. Every second matters. If people scroll away too soon, your video is essentially dead. But if they stay engaged, rewatch, like, or comment, the algorithm takes notice, marking your content as valuable and promoting it to even more users. The key isn't just to make videos—it's to make videos that YouTube *wants* to promote. The creators who understand this simple fact are the ones who dominate the platform.

Take, for example, a beginner creator who struggled to get even 100 views on his Shorts. At first, he assumed that success was random, that going viral was purely luck. But as he analyzed top-performing videos, he realized a pattern—successful creators weren't just making good content; they were strategically structuring their Shorts to maximize engagement and retention. He refined his approach, focusing on gripping hooks, seamless storytelling, and unexpected twists that forced viewers to stay until the end. The results were undeniable. Within months, his Shorts went from barely reaching 100 views to consistently hitting tens of thousands, then hundreds of thousands, and eventually millions.

This is the reality of YouTube Shorts. It's not about who has the most expensive equipment or the biggest following—it's about who understands the game. And once you learn how to play it, you'll never look at content creation the same way again.

# Chapter 2: Choosing the Right Topics That Always Work

The foundation of every viral YouTube Short starts with understanding *who* you're creating for. Many aspiring creators make the mistake of producing content based on what they *think* will perform well, without ever considering their audience's preferences. But virality isn't about what *you* want—it's about delivering exactly what your viewers crave.

To do this, you need to identify your ideal audience. Who are they? What interests them? What type of content keeps them engaged? The easiest way to find out is by looking at existing trends. Study the big channels in your niche—the ones consistently pulling in millions of views. What do their most popular Shorts have in common? Is it the humor, the storytelling, the suspense? Take note of the topics, styles, and formats that repeatedly generate high engagement. If a particular type of video has already gone viral, there's a good chance it will work again with the right execution.

But don't just copy—analyze. Go beyond the surface and break down the mechanics of these viral Shorts. How do they start? What hooks do they use? How do they maintain interest throughout the video? Watch with the mindset of a creator, not just a viewer. Every viral Short leaves behind clues, a formula hidden beneath the entertainment. If you can decode it, you can replicate its success in your own unique way.

The key is to bridge the gap between what's already working and what makes *you* unique as a creator. By researching viral content while staying true to your own voice, you create a winning combination—content that resonates with your audience while standing out in a crowded space. And when you truly understand what your viewers love, every Short you post becomes a step closer to hitting that viral jackpot.

Every successful YouTube Shorts creator faces a crucial decision—should they chase trends or focus on evergreen content? Both have their advantages, but understanding how each works is the key to maximizing long-term growth.

Trending content is powerful. When a topic is hot, the algorithm is already primed to push related videos, meaning your Short has a higher chance of getting picked up quickly. Trending challenges, viral memes, or major events can generate a flood of instant views, skyrocketing your reach in a short period. However, trends are fleeting. A viral Short today can become irrelevant within weeks, leaving you constantly searching for the next big thing.

Evergreen content, on the other hand, has lasting value. These

7

are Shorts that continue to get views months or even years after being posted. Educational tips, life hacks, motivational stories, and universally relatable moments never go out of style. They may not explode overnight like trending content, but they build consistent traction over time, steadily increasing your views and subscriber count. The smartest creators strike a balance—leveraging trends for quick bursts of virality while investing in evergreen content for sustained growth.

No matter which type of content you choose, the real key to virality lies in the *Interest Hook* formula. A Short only succeeds if it grabs attention within the first few seconds. People scroll fast, and if your opening isn't compelling, they'll swipe away without a second thought. The best hooks spark curiosity and leave viewers with questions they *need* answered.

For example, instead of saying, "Here's how to get more views on YouTube," a stronger hook would be, "I posted the same Short twice, and one got 100 views while the other hit 1 million. Here's why." This instantly sparks intrigue—why did one succeed and the other fail? The viewer *has* to keep watching to find out.

The most effective hooks create a sense of mystery, excitement, or urgency. They tease just enough information to pull the viewer in but leave out the full answer, ensuring they stay engaged. Mastering this formula is what separates forgettable Shorts from those that keep audiences watching until the very last second—because once they're hooked, the algorithm does the rest.

4

# Chapter 3: The Art of Storytelling in Shorts

Many creators assume that storytelling is reserved for long-form videos, but in reality, it's the backbone of every viral YouTube Short. The difference? You have less than 60 seconds to capture attention, build intrigue, and deliver a satisfying payoff—all while keeping viewers engaged. The best Shorts don't just present information; they take the audience on a journey. Whether it's a suspenseful moment, an unexpected twist, or a step-by-step buildup to a big reveal, great storytelling makes a Short impossible to scroll past.

At its core, a compelling Short follows a simple structure: Hook, Progression, and Climax (HPC). The *Hook* grabs attention instantly—often by sparking curiosity, making a bold statement, or presenting a problem that demands a solution. The *Progression* keeps the viewer engaged by building suspense or showcasing a transformation. Finally, the *Climax* delivers the payoff, ensuring the audience feels rewarded for sticking around.

One of the biggest mistakes creators make is revealing too much, too soon. If the payoff happens within the first few seconds, there's no reason for viewers to keep watching. Retention drops, and the algorithm takes note, limiting the video's reach. The secret to maintaining engagement is controlled pacing. A well-crafted Short teases just enough information to make the viewer crave more, stretching the anticipation until the very last moment.

Imagine a video titled: *"The Secret Behind Every Viral YouTube Short."* If, within the first five seconds, the creator says, "The secret is high retention," the mystery is gone, and viewers will swipe away. Instead, a strong Short would open with, "Every viral Short follows a hidden formula, but most creators don't realize it. Watch closely, and you'll never struggle with views again." This sets up a question—*What's the formula?*—that keeps the audience engaged until they get the answer at the end.

Mastering storytelling, even in short-form content, is what separates forgettable videos from viral sensations. A well-structured narrative not only keeps viewers watching but also increases their likelihood of engaging—commenting, liking, and sharing—which signals to YouTube's algorithm that your Short deserves even more reach.

The key to keeping viewers hooked on a YouTube Short isn't just about having an interesting topic—it's about *how* you deliver it. The most successful creators understand the psychology of *anticipation* and use it to their advantage. In short-form content, where attention spans are at their shortest, mastering the art of delayed gratification can mean the difference between a viral hit and a forgettable video.

Building anticipation is all about controlling the flow of information. If you reveal everything too quickly, there's no reason for viewers to stay. But if you tease just enough to spark curiosity, they *have* to keep watching to get the answer. This strategy works because it plays into a simple psychological principle: the human brain *hates* unfinished stories. When a question is posed, an incomplete action is shown, or a problem is presented without an immediate solution, the audience feels compelled to stick around until they get closure.

Take a look at some viral examples that execute this perfectly. One creator starts a Short with: *"I found a wallet on the ground. What happened next completely shocked me."* Instantly, the viewer is left wondering—*Did they return it? Was there something weird inside?*—and that curiosity keeps them watching. Another Short follows the structure of a challenge video: *"I'm about to test a viral life hack that claims to open any lock without a key. Will it actually work? Let's find out."* Again, the setup creates suspense, and the only way to get the answer is to watch through to the end.

A perfect real-world example of anticipation-driven storytelling is the viral Short about having a snowball fight in the desert. The creator immediately hooks the audience by making an unexpected claim: *"I want to be the first person to have a snowball fight in the desert."* This statement alone sparks intrigue—*How will they get snow? Is this even possible?*—and the viewer is now invested. Instead of rushing to the payoff, the video takes them on a journey, showing obstacles along the way: *"It's too hot. The sand won't form snowballs. We don't have any snow."* Each challenge builds anticipation until the final moment when the mission is completed, delivering a satisfying climax.

This same storytelling approach can be applied to any niche. Whether you're making educational content, reaction videos, or challenges, structuring your Shorts around *anticipation* will naturally boost retention. And once you get people watching till the end, YouTube's algorithm will do the rest—pushing your content to even more viewers, ensuring your next Short has the potential to go viral.

# Chapter 4: The HPC Formula for Viral Shorts

A t the heart of every viral YouTube Short lies a simple yet powerful storytelling framework known as **HPC**—Hook, Progression, and Climax. This formula is the secret behind high-retention videos that the algorithm loves to push. Understanding and applying HPC ensures that your Shorts captivate audiences from the first second to the last, increasing watch time, engagement, and overall performance.

The **Hook** is the most critical part of any Short. Within the first 3–5 seconds, you must capture attention and give viewers a reason to stay. If the opening isn't compelling, they'll scroll away, and your video won't get the momentum it needs. A strong hook achieves two things: it sparks curiosity and leaves the audience with questions they *need* answered. For example, a creator might open with: *"I spent 24 hours in a haunted house, and what I saw changed my life forever."* Instantly, the viewer is hooked—*What did they see? Was it real?*—and they feel compelled to keep watching. The key is to create a sense of urgency or intrigue that stops people from swiping past.

Once you've captured attention, the **Progression** phase keeps viewers engaged. This is where you develop the story, add challenges, and build anticipation. A great Short unfolds like a mini-adventure, with each moment pulling the audience further in. Take the viral example of the snowball fight in the desert. After the hook, the creator doesn't immediately reveal the solution. Instead, they introduce obstacles—*It's too hot. The sand won't form snowballs. There's no snow.* This keeps the audience engaged because they *need* to see how the problem will be solved. Progression is about *pacing*—keeping the story moving without giving away the climax too soon.

Finally, the **Climax** is where the payoff happens. This is the moment viewers have been waiting for—the mystery is solved, the challenge is completed, or the transformation is revealed. A weak climax can ruin an otherwise great Short, but a satisfying one rewards the audience for staying, making them more likely to engage, comment, and share. In the snowball fight example, the climax is when the characters finally gather enough snow and start throwing it in the desert. It delivers on the promise set in the hook and closes the story with a fulfilling ending.

Mastering HPC ensures that your Shorts don't just attract views—they *hold* attention. And retention is everything. The longer people watch, the more the algorithm pushes your content, leading to explosive growth. Whether you're making educational videos, entertainment, or challenges, structuring your Shorts around **Hook, Progression, and Climax** is the ultimate formula for virality.

The magic of HPC isn't just theoretical—it's a proven strategy that top YouTube Shorts creators use to propel their videos to viral status. By consistently applying the **Hook, Progression, and Climax** formula, these creators manage to capture attention, keep viewers hooked, and deliver a satisfying payoff that drives massive engagement. Let's look at how they apply this method and break down how you can implement it in your own Shorts.

## Real-World Application – How Top Shorts Creators Use This Method

Top creators are masters of the HPC method, with each of their Shorts structured in a way that maximizes engagement. Consider the YouTube Shorts sensation that starts with a bold claim: *"I'm about to do something no one has ever done before."* This line isn't just an introduction—it's a hook that piques curiosity. Viewers are immediately wondering, *What is this creator about to do? Is it really unique?* This curiosity sets the stage for the rest of the video, and the first few seconds are designed to keep viewers locked in.

The **Progression** comes next. Top creators don't reveal everything immediately. They start building the story with small clues or escalating challenges. For example, in a viral challenge Short, the creator might say, *"But first, I need to gather all the materials, and it won't be easy..."* This builds anticipation, adding small hurdles along the way to keep the audience invested. The audience wants to see if the creator will succeed, fail, or discover something unexpected. By stringing these small, intriguing moments together, top creators create a narrative that keeps viewers watching to the end.

Then comes the **Climax**. This is the moment the viewer has been waiting for—the big reveal, the punchline, the solution to the problem, or the completion of the challenge. A well-executed climax gives the audience what they were promised in the hook, but it might add an unexpected twist to keep things fresh. Imagine a creator who promises to build a super-powered rocket launcher out of household items. After the progression where they gather the materials and explain the process, the climax would show them firing the rocket and achieving something extraordinary. The payoff has to live up to the setup to ensure maximum satisfaction.

### Step-by-Step Implementation – Crafting Your Shorts Using HPC

Now that you understand how top creators use HPC, let's break down how you can implement this strategy step by step to craft your own viral Shorts.

1. **Create an Attention-Grabbing Hook:**The first few seconds of your Short are the most important. Your hook must make viewers stop scrolling and make them *want* to see more. Focus on curiosity, surprise, or an intriguing question. For example, instead of a generic intro like, *"Here's a life hack,"* you could say, *"I'm going to show you a life hack that could change your life—if it actually works."* The subtle doubt creates curiosity and makes viewers stick around to see if the hack works.

2. **Build Progression with Small Hurdles or Revela-**

**tions**:Once you've caught their attention, don't give away everything at once. The progression phase should move the story forward with small challenges, surprises, or revelations. If your video is instructional, walk the audience through the steps without revealing the final result too early. If it's a challenge, build suspense by showing setbacks or unexpected twists. Keep the pacing quick but make sure every moment adds value or raises the stakes.

3. **Deliver the Climax and Keep It Satisfying**:The climax should be the payoff the audience has been waiting for. Whether it's an epic moment, a surprise ending, or the solution to a problem, make sure it delivers on the promise made in the hook. But here's the secret: leave room for the unexpected. The best climaxes don't just end predictably; they offer something that exceeds expectations. For example, if your Short was about solving a tricky puzzle, don't just reveal the solution. Maybe throw in a small twist, like revealing how you solved it in a completely unconventional way.

4. **Refine and Polish**:As you experiment with HPC, make sure to refine each part of the formula. Your hook should be snappy and intriguing, the progression should flow naturally, and the climax should deliver the ultimate payoff. Pay attention to pacing—if your progression feels too slow or rushed, adjust the timing to keep the audience engaged. Add elements like quick cuts, suspenseful music, or on-screen captions to enhance the viewer experience.

5. **Test and Tweak**:The beauty of YouTube Shorts is that you can experiment and see what works. Test different types of hooks, progressions, and climaxes to find out what

resonates with your audience. Look at your analytics to see where people are dropping off, and adjust accordingly. If viewers are leaving too early, try making your hook more engaging. If your retention drops after the midpoint, think about how you can add more tension or curiosity in the progression phase.

By following these steps and using the HPC method, you'll be able to create YouTube Shorts that not only grab attention but also hold it all the way through to the climax. With practice, you'll be well on your way to mastering the art of viral Shorts and building a loyal audience that can't wait for your next video.

# Chapter 5: Mastering Editing & Structure for Maximum Engagement

I n the world of YouTube Shorts, great content alone isn't enough. How you present that content can make all the difference between a video that gets a few views and one that goes viral. **Editing** plays a crucial role in retention—keeping your viewers glued to the screen from start to finish. Without the right editing techniques, even the most captivating hook can lose its power, and a well-constructed progression can fall flat. Here's how editing works to maintain engagement and keep your audience watching until the very end.

### The Role of Editing in Retention – How Fast Cuts and Pacing Keep Viewers Watching

In the fast-paced world of YouTube Shorts, viewers have a short attention span. If your video drags on or feels too slow, they'll swipe away, and your chance of going viral is gone. Fast cuts and a sharp sense of pacing are key to holding attention and keeping your Shorts dynamic.

The first element to focus on is **fast cuts**. These are rapid transitions between scenes, action shots, or visual changes that keep the energy high. Each cut should feel purposeful—either to reveal something new, increase the pace, or change the visual scenery. This prevents the viewer from becoming bored or losing interest. Think of it like the beat in a song—the quicker and more rhythmic the cuts, the more engaging the video becomes.

However, **pacing** is just as important as cutting quickly. You don't want the cuts to be so rapid that the viewer can't follow what's happening. Instead, pacing should be about maintaining a balance between moments of action and quieter pauses that allow the story to breathe. For example, after a fast-paced segment where something exciting happens, you might want to slow things down for just a second to let the viewer catch up. This creates contrast and keeps the audience engaged throughout. A good pacing strategy involves knowing when to accelerate the speed of cuts and when to let a scene linger for a moment longer, adding anticipation or building suspense.

If done correctly, this editing rhythm will ensure that your Short moves fluidly from one moment to the next, never giving the viewer a reason to look away. In fact, when the pace is right, viewers will subconsciously feel like they're in a constant state of expectation, eagerly waiting for what happens next.

### Effective Captioning – Making Content More Engaging and Accessible

While editing can enhance retention, **captioning** takes it a step further by making your content more engaging, accessible, and easy to consume. In today's world, many people watch videos without sound—whether they're on a crowded train, at work, or simply not wanting to disturb others. If you don't use captions, you're potentially missing out on a massive portion of your audience. But captioning does more than just provide accessibility—it can also be an incredibly powerful storytelling tool.

Start by using captions to **highlight key points** in your Shorts. Whether it's a witty comment, a surprising fact, or an important statement, captions can emphasize the moments you want the viewer to remember. For example, instead of just saying a punchline, show it in bold text on the screen for added impact. This makes the content more engaging for viewers, helping them follow the narrative or enjoy a joke more thoroughly.

Moreover, captions allow you to cater to **a wider audience** by being more inclusive. Many people, including those with hearing impairments, rely on captions to enjoy video content. By adding clear, concise captions, you make your content accessible to everyone, ensuring no one misses out. In fact, studies have shown that videos with captions tend to receive higher engagement rates because they appeal to a larger audience and keep people watching longer.

The way you style your captions also matters. To keep things interesting, vary your text size, color, and animation. Use bolder text for important moments or fun sound effects to make your captions feel more dynamic. This isn't just about accessibility—it's about amplifying the viewing experience. By adding this extra layer of visual stimulation, you're not just telling a story; you're enhancing it.

Editing and captioning work hand-in-hand to boost engagement and retention in YouTube Shorts. Fast cuts and pacing keep viewers intrigued and prevent them from losing interest, while effective captioning ensures that your content is accessible and keeps your audience connected to the story. When both are used strategically, they create a seamless, high-quality viewing experience that keeps your audience watching and coming back for more.

When it comes to YouTube Shorts, the power of **audio** is often underestimated. In fact, your choice of music and sound effects can dramatically influence the mood, pace, and emotional impact of your video. Audio isn't just something that plays in the background—it's an integral part of storytelling that can elevate your content in ways visuals alone cannot.

## The Music & Sound Effect Strategy – Why Audio Choices Can Make or Break a Short

Imagine watching a video with no sound—no music, no sound effects—just visuals. While it may be technically watchable, it lacks the depth and engagement that audio brings to the table. Music and sound effects are what create **atmosphere** and **emotion** in a video. They set the tone, amplify moments of drama, excitement, or humor, and guide the viewer's emotional journey. Without the right audio, your Short may fall flat.

For starters, **music** helps to establish the pace of your video.

Fast-paced, energetic tracks will add a sense of urgency and excitement, while slower, more mellow music will create a laid-back or contemplative vibe. This alignment between the music and the visuals is crucial to keeping the viewer engaged. Music should complement the action on screen—think of it as a soundtrack to the narrative you're telling.

Equally important are **sound effects**—the little nuances that can make a video feel more dynamic and immersive. A punchline lands harder with the right sound effect, and a dramatic reveal is made even more thrilling with a well-timed sound cue. The **impact of sound effects** lies in their ability to punctuate moments and elevate simple actions, turning them into more memorable experiences. Whether it's a whoosh when something moves quickly, a chime for a dramatic reveal, or a fun pop sound for comedic moments, sound effects enhance the experience in a way visuals alone cannot.

However, balance is key. Too much music or an overuse of sound effects can overwhelm the viewer. You want your audio choices to complement the visuals, not overshadow them. Finding that sweet spot where music and sound effects subtly enhance the experience is essential to crafting a viral Short.

## Visual Storytelling – Using Graphics, Zooms, and Transitions to Enhance Engagement

While music and audio create the emotional undercurrent of your video, **visual storytelling** is where you capture the viewer's attention and guide them through the narrative. The **visuals** in your Short should do more than just show what's happening—they should actively contribute to the story, enhance engagement, and keep the viewer interested.

One powerful tool in visual storytelling is the **use of graphics**. Whether it's text overlays, icons, or animated visuals, graphics can be used to emphasize key points, clarify information, or add a layer of fun. For example, if you're explaining a step-by-step process, a graphic showing each step can help reinforce the message. If you're telling a joke, adding a playful graphic or emoji can enhance the humor. Graphics should be clear, visually appealing, and aligned with the tone of the video, not just thrown in randomly.

**Zooms** are another visual technique that can add emphasis and focus to your Shorts. A zoom-in can create a sense of intimacy or urgency, highlighting an important detail or moment. Whether you're zooming in on a reaction, an object, or an expression, this simple move can dramatically alter the viewer's perception and make the moment feel more intense. Conversely, a zoom-out can give a broader perspective or provide context, pulling the viewer back to see the bigger picture.

Finally, **transitions** between shots play a crucial role in maintaining engagement. Smooth transitions ensure that your Short flows seamlessly, keeping the viewer's attention on the story without any awkward pauses or jarring cuts. Whether it's a swipe, fade, or creative transition (like a jump cut or whip pan), transitions help maintain the rhythm and pace of the video. They should be used thoughtfully and in line with the style of your video, enhancing the narrative rather than distracting from it.

Just like with editing and audio, visual storytelling works best when it's purposeful and intentional. Every zoom, transition, and graphic should add value to the narrative you're telling. When done right, these visual elements enhance engagement by keeping the viewer visually intrigued and emotionally invested in your Short.

Together, **audio choices** and **visual storytelling** form the backbone of a highly engaging Short. They're the secret ingredients that take your content from good to great, adding depth, emotion, and excitement. If you master these strategies, your Shorts will not only capture the viewer's attention but hold it until the very last frame. Whether through music that sets the mood, sound effects that punctuate the action, or visuals that enhance the story, these elements work in harmony to create a viewing experience that leaves a lasting impact.

# Chapter 6: Posting Strategy & Growth Hacks

One of the most crucial aspects of YouTube Shorts that many creators overlook is the **timing** of their posts. You might have crafted the perfect video, with an attention-grabbing hook and a killer story, but if you post it at the wrong time, all that effort could go to waste. The **timing of your posts** plays a significant role in how well they perform, as it determines when your audience is most likely to see and engage with your content. Fortunately, **YouTube provides powerful analytics tools** to help you understand the best time to post based on when your audience is most active.

## The Best Time to Post – How Analytics Reveal When Your Audience is Most Active

Think of it like fishing. You could have the best bait in the world, but if you're fishing in a pond where there are no fish, you're not going to catch anything. Similarly, posting your Shorts when your audience isn't online is like casting your line into an empty pond. You need to know when your audience is most active so that your videos have the best chance of being seen and engaged with.

YouTube's analytics provide valuable insights that reveal when your audience is most active. By going to the "**Audience**" tab in your YouTube Studio, you can see a graph that indicates the times and days when your viewers are online. This data gives you a clear understanding of **when your audience is most likely to engage** with your content. Posting during these peak times increases the chances of your Shorts being shown to a larger audience, which in turn boosts the likelihood of virality.

It's important to note that this data varies from creator to creator. While mornings might work best for some, afternoons or evenings might be the sweet spot for others. This is where understanding your own **audience's behavior** comes into play. **Experimenting** with different posting times and comparing the results can help you fine-tune your posting schedule to maximize visibility.

Analytics aren't just about the best time of day to post, though. They can also reveal patterns in **day of the week**. Some creators find that posting on weekends yields better results, while others see more success during the workweek. It's all about finding the time frame that works for you and your specific audience.

## How Often Should You Post? – Finding the Right Balance Between Quality and Frequency

When it comes to posting on YouTube Shorts, consistency is key. However, there's always the question of **how often you should post**. Posting too frequently can lead to burnout and lower-quality content, while posting too infrequently can cause you to lose momentum and visibility. So, what's the sweet spot?

The answer is: it depends. Every creator has to find a balance between **quality and frequency** that works for them. Some creators may find that posting **twice a week** allows them to maintain a high level of quality while still staying consistent. Others may prefer posting **once a day**, ensuring that their content is regularly seen without compromising the production value.

It's tempting to post as much as possible, but **posting too often** can be detrimental. When you upload content in quick succession, YouTube may not have enough time to fully analyze each video before the next one goes up. As a result, some videos might get lost in the shuffle, and your overall engagement rate might drop.

On the flip side, **posting too little** can hurt your growth. If you don't post regularly, your audience may forget about you, or you might not be giving YouTube's algorithm enough of a chance to push your content. **Consistency** helps you stay in the algorithm's favor and ensures that your channel remains active in the eyes of your viewers.

Ultimately, it's about finding a posting schedule that fits with your content creation process. **Focus on quality**, but don't let perfectionism hold you back. Find a pace that allows you to maintain your standards while also ensuring that your channel stays active and your audience stays engaged.

**Experimentation** is key. Don't be afraid to test different posting frequencies and observe how your audience responds. If you find that posting once per day leads to higher engagement and better results, stick with it. On the other hand, if you feel that quality suffers when posting too frequently, try scaling back and see how that affects your views and engagement.

Balancing quality and frequency is a delicate act, but once you find the rhythm that works for you, it can make a huge difference in your success on YouTube Shorts. The key is to stay consistent and flexible, always adapting your strategy based on the feedback you get from your audience and analytics.

In the world of YouTube Shorts, **momentum** is everything. The ability to keep your channel growing, even when you don't see immediate results, is one of the most critical factors for sustained success. **Consistency** doesn't just apply to your posting schedule; it's also about maintaining a constant flow of quality content that keeps your audience engaged and coming back for more.

## The Momentum Factor – Why Consistency Is Key to Sustained Growth

Building momentum on YouTube is much like building a snowball. At first, it may seem like you're pushing a small ball up a steep hill, but over time, as you keep rolling that snowball, it gathers size, speed, and power. Similarly, when you consistently post quality Shorts, YouTube's algorithm begins to recognize your channel as active and reliable, and it starts to push your content to more and more viewers.

Consistency does more than just boost your visibility—it builds trust with your audience. The more often you post, the more opportunities you create for your viewers to interact with your content. **Engagement**, which is a key metric that drives YouTube's algorithm, grows exponentially when your followers see that you are consistently delivering content that resonates with them. The more they watch, the more they'll interact, share, and recommend your videos to others.

Consistency also helps you stay relevant. In an ever-changing digital landscape, new trends and challenges come and go in the blink of an eye. By maintaining a steady posting schedule, you ensure that you're always in the loop, ready to capitalize on new opportunities as they arise. This also prevents you from losing momentum, which can be a common issue for creators who take extended breaks or post infrequently.

The power of momentum isn't just about posting every day, though—it's about posting with purpose. The consistency of your content quality, tone, and focus will build a loyal audience.

This audience begins to anticipate your next video, which in turn drives **retention**, another essential factor for success. As your channel grows, so will the snowball effect of your efforts—views increase, subscribers rise, and eventually, virality becomes more of a certainty than a chance.

## Avoiding Common Pitfalls – Mistakes That Limit Your Reach and How to Fix Them

The road to viral success on YouTube Shorts isn't always smooth, and many creators unknowingly fall into common pitfalls that severely limit their reach. Fortunately, these mistakes are avoidable, and by learning from them, you can save yourself from unnecessary setbacks.

One of the biggest mistakes creators make is **ignoring their audience's preferences**. Often, creators get caught up in what they *think* will go viral instead of focusing on what their audience is already engaging with. You need to **know your audience**—what they enjoy, what they are passionate about, and what kind of content keeps them engaged. It's not enough to simply chase trends or create random content; you need to ensure that every video you produce aligns with what your target viewers want to see.

Another common pitfall is **poor video quality**. While YouTube Shorts is designed for quick, casual content, that doesn't mean quality can be sacrificed. Low production values can easily turn viewers off, and in many cases, it'll affect your retention rate. Keep in mind that **attention spans are short**, and viewers will scroll away at the slightest sign of poor audio, bad lighting, or unpolished visuals. Investing in even simple upgrades like better lighting or clearer audio can make a huge difference in how your content is received.

**Not optimizing for the algorithm** is another mistake that many creators make. Remember, YouTube's algorithm isn't about luck—it's about engaging content that keeps viewers watching. If you're not paying attention to key elements like your **title, thumbnail, and first few seconds of your video**, you might be missing out on views. The algorithm relies heavily on **engagement metrics**, so without effective optimization, even your best videos may not reach as wide an audience as they could.

Another pitfall is **overposting or underposting**. As mentioned earlier, consistency is crucial, but there's a fine line between posting too much and posting too little. Posting too frequently can reduce the quality of your content, and posting too rarely can cause you to lose momentum. Find a schedule that works for you—whether that's once a day, a few times a week, or even less frequent but highly polished content.

Lastly, a common mistake is **ignoring the power of editing**. It's easy to think that YouTube Shorts is all about the idea, but **editing** is what makes your video come alive. Without good pacing, cuts, captions, and transitions, even the most interesting topic can fall flat. Learn how to edit your videos effectively to keep the pace fast and the audience engaged. **Add captions for accessibility**, use cuts to remove unnecessary filler, and don't forget to add some visual and audio effects to keep things exciting.

The key to avoiding these pitfalls is **self-awareness and continuous learning**. Pay attention to your performance, observe what works, and be ready to adjust your approach when necessary. Every mistake is a chance to improve, and every successful video is a step closer to creating a thriving YouTube Shorts channel. By avoiding these common traps and focusing on creating value for your audience, you'll be setting yourself up for long-term success.

# 8

# Chapter 7: Learning from the Best & Avoiding Mistakes

Reverse Engineering Success – Studying Viral Creators for Hidden Insights

The success of viral creators on YouTube Shorts is far from accidental. While some might argue that virality is simply a matter of luck, the truth is that the most successful creators have **mastered the art** of reverse engineering their content. By studying top-performing Shorts and analyzing what makes them tick, they've cracked the code on what works and what doesn't. The beauty of **reverse engineering** is that it allows you to learn from others' successes and failures without having to reinvent the wheel.

The first step in this process is identifying viral creators within your niche. Look at what makes their content so appealing. Is it their use of humor, the way they tell stories, or how they engage with their audience? Pay attention to the structure of their videos, how they hook the audience within the first few seconds, and how they keep viewers watching until the end. But don't just stop there—look deeper. How are they editing their videos? What kind of transitions and effects do they use? How do they keep the pacing quick and the energy high?

Reverse engineering allows you to pinpoint **patterns** and **strategies** that work. For example, you might notice that many viral creators use the same kind of music or sound effects, or they often leverage trending topics that resonate with their audience. Once you've identified these elements, you can start applying them to your own content, using the same principles while putting your unique spin on things.

Studying viral creators also helps you recognize the **elements of a great hook**. The first few seconds of a YouTube Short are the most important, and creators who go viral often excel in this area. They understand the significance of grabbing attention right away and know how to make the viewer want to keep watching. By paying attention to how these creators construct their hooks, you can learn valuable lessons that will help you increase your own engagement and retention rates.

Additionally, it's important to keep in mind that reverse engineering doesn't mean copying. The goal is to **understand the formula** behind successful Shorts and adapt it to your own style. In other words, study what works, but don't be afraid to **make it your own**.

## The Power of Imitation & Innovation – Learning from Others While Keeping Originality

One of the most powerful ways to grow on YouTube Shorts is through the **combination of imitation and innovation**. This approach is rooted in the idea that success leaves clues. By observing what successful creators are doing, you can **learn from their strategies** and apply those lessons to your own content. However, there's a fine line between imitation and outright copying, and it's important to find your own voice while still benefiting from others' experiences.

**Imitation** is the foundation of learning. Think about it: every successful creator, artist, or entrepreneur has had to learn from someone else. The greats didn't become great by avoiding the work of others—they studied their idols and learned from their strategies, whether it was how they edited, how they structured their stories, or how they engaged with their audience. This principle holds true for YouTube Shorts creators as well. By observing what works for others, you can quickly find **shortcuts** to success, saving yourself from unnecessary trial and error.

But imitation alone won't get you far. While learning from successful creators is essential, you must **innovate** in order to stand out. Innovation is about putting your **unique twist** on what's already working. It's about using the insights you've gained through studying others and making them your own. This could be through a unique storytelling approach, using different editing techniques, or adding a fresh perspective to popular trends. **Originality** is what will differentiate you from the crowd and help you carve out your niche.

Remember, YouTube Shorts is a platform driven by creativity. As much as you can learn from others, it's crucial that you don't lose sight of your own unique voice and personality. Your audience is looking for **authenticity**—they want to see you, not a copy of someone else. So while it's helpful to follow successful trends and strategies, always make sure to infuse your personal touch into your content.

In the end, the power of **imitation and innovation** is a balancing act. By studying viral creators, you can shortcut your learning process, but by infusing your personal originality into your videos, you'll ensure your growth is sustainable and unique. The creators who truly stand out on YouTube Shorts are the ones who are able to **learn from others while staying true to their own style**. That's the secret to building a long-term, successful presence on the platform.

## Analyzing Failing Shorts – Spotting and Fixing Engagement-Killing Mistakes

Not every YouTube Short is going to go viral, and that's okay. In fact, the key to long-term success is **learning from failure** and refining your content based on the lessons you learn from each attempt. Understanding why a Short didn't perform as well as expected is crucial to improving your future content. Fortunately, there are specific mistakes that creators commonly make, and by spotting them, you can **fix them** and avoid repeating the same missteps.

One of the most significant engagement-killing mistakes is **lack of a strong hook**. If the first few seconds of your Short don't capture attention, viewers will quickly swipe away. You need to make sure that your hook is **immediately intriguing**—something that makes the viewer stop scrolling and want to know more. If your hook is too weak or unclear, your views will plummet. Re-evaluating the first moments of your video is a good place to start.

Another common mistake is **poor pacing**. In the fast-paced world of Shorts, if your content feels slow or meandering, it's going to lose viewers quickly. Keep the energy high and ensure that your video doesn't feel like it drags. If there are lulls or filler moments, consider trimming them. A short, sharp, and exciting progression will help maintain the viewers' attention from start to finish.

A mistake many creators overlook is the **lack of a payoff**. A lot of Shorts fizzle out because they don't deliver on the promise made at the start of the video. If your hook gets the viewer interested but there's no real payoff or resolution, they'll feel unsatisfied and less likely to watch your future content. Always ensure that your content follows through on what you promised in the opening, whether it's an answer, a solution, or a funny twist.

Additionally, consider **audience retention**: if viewers are dropping off at the 5-second mark, it could mean the pacing is off or the content is not as compelling as it should be. If they're dropping off right before the climax, maybe you need a more exciting or satisfying payoff to keep them invested. **Analyzing** where people lose interest will give you valuable insights into where your Shorts are going wrong and what you can fix.

When analyzing failing Shorts, it's important to take a step back and be objective. Don't get discouraged by a poor performance—**view it as a learning opportunity**. By fixing engagement-killing mistakes, you'll be much more equipped to create content that sticks and gets the attention it deserves.

## How to Pivot When Shorts Flop – Strategies for Refining and Improving Content

When your Shorts don't perform as expected, it can be disheartening, but it's also an opportunity to **pivot and adjust your strategy**. The beauty of YouTube Shorts is that you don't need to wait long to get feedback. The results are immediate, and with each video, you can **test new ideas, approaches, and content styles** to see what resonates with your audience. The key is not to get stuck in a rut but to **refine your approach** continuously.

One of the first things you can do when a Short flops is to **analyze the analytics**. Pay attention to metrics like **view duration**, **engagement rates**, and **audience retention**. Where did people drop off? Did they stop watching at the hook, the progression, or the climax? This will give you the exact moments where your content lost them, so you know where to focus your improvements. For example, if your retention rate drops after the first five seconds, you need to improve your hook to make it stronger.

If your video is being ignored despite having a strong hook, it could be because of the **topic choice**. Sometimes, a viral formula or trend just isn't resonating with your audience, and that's okay. The solution? **Experiment with new topics**. Look at what's trending in your niche and ask yourself, "What can I do differently?" Instead of copying what's popular, add a unique angle that will catch people's attention. Focus on what's interesting or valuable to your audience, not just what's trending in the moment.

Also, **switch up your content structure** if you find that a certain style or format isn't performing well. Try experimenting with different pacing, editing styles, or video lengths. Sometimes, changing your approach or combining multiple styles can yield fresh results. For example, if you've been making purely educational content, try incorporating humor, or if you've been doing purely entertainment-based Shorts, experiment with adding value through tips or advice.

Another effective strategy is to **engage with your community**. Ask for feedback from your audience through comments or polls. You can even ask what kind of content they want to see more of. Involving your audience in the creative process not only gives you valuable insights, but it also creates a sense of community around your content.

Finally, don't be afraid to **take risks**. If something isn't working, try something completely new. Creativity thrives when you step outside your comfort zone and try unexpected combinations of styles, trends, and ideas. You won't know what truly works unless you give yourself the freedom to experiment and explore different approaches.

The important thing is that you never stop evolving. When one Short flops, don't throw in the towel; instead, **pivot, learn, and improve**. By consistently refining your content, you'll gradually hone in on what works for your audience, and success will follow.

# 9

# Conclusion: Your Roadmap to YouTube Shorts Success

As we reach the final page of this journey, it's important to pause and reflect on everything we've covered. You now have a **complete roadmap** for creating YouTube Shorts that don't just get views—they go viral. But the road to success is not one of chance or random luck. Instead, it's built on a foundation of **strategic effort**, continuous learning, and constant adaptation. Success in the world of Shorts is the result of a thoughtful, calculated approach, and now you have the tools to execute that plan.

## Final Thoughts & Encouragement – The Reality of Success Through Strategic Effort

The journey to mastering YouTube Shorts isn't instantaneous. It requires patience, perseverance, and a willingness to refine your craft. But remember this—**virality is not a random event**; it's a **calculated outcome** that follows a proven formula. By implementing the strategies laid out in this book, you're setting yourself up for success, one Short at a time.

There will be times when a video doesn't perform as well as expected, but that's part of the process. Every creator goes through it. **Failure is simply feedback**, and it's through these moments of trial and error that the best content is born. Don't get discouraged if things don't immediately blow up—**keep testing, keep improving, and keep creating**.

The reality is that virality isn't about luck; it's about mastering the art of storytelling, understanding your audience, and consistently improving your content. With the knowledge you've gained here, you are now equipped to take your content to the next level. **The success you desire is within your reach**, and the only thing standing between you and that success is **action**.

## Your Action Plan – Step-by-Step Execution to Start Creating Viral Shorts

It's time to roll up your sleeves and put everything you've learned into action. Here's a step-by-step breakdown to help you **kickstart your journey** toward viral YouTube Shorts:

1. **Identify Your Niche and Audience**: Begin by defining who your target audience is. Research what topics and trends are resonating with them, and identify the type of content they're actively engaging with.
2. **Craft a Strong Hook**: The first few seconds of your Short are crucial. Develop a compelling hook that immediately grabs attention. Ask yourself, "What will make the viewer stop scrolling and want to watch more?"
3. **Build Progression and Pacing**: Keep the energy high by creating a clear progression from start to finish. Every moment should build toward the climax, maintaining the viewer's interest throughout.
4. **Focus on the Climax**: The payoff is everything. Make sure that the conclusion of your Short delivers exactly what was promised in the hook. Viewers need to feel satisfied by the end.
5. **Perfect Your Editing**: Fast cuts, strategic pacing, and dynamic transitions are key. Experiment with different editing styles and find what keeps viewers engaged.
6. **Analyze Analytics and Feedback**: After posting, analyze your performance. What's working? What isn't? Adjust your strategy based on the data, and continue learning from your audience.
7. **Consistency is Key**: Develop a posting schedule that

allows you to upload regularly without compromising quality. The more you post, the more you increase your chances of finding success.

8. **Experiment and Innovate**: Don't be afraid to try new things. Explore different content styles, trends, and approaches. Stay ahead of the curve by always evolving your content.

By following these steps, you're well on your way to becoming a Shorts creator who consistently delivers content that captures attention and drives massive engagement.

## Next Steps – Resources and Additional Learning to Keep Improving

Now that you've laid the groundwork for success, it's time to **keep learning and improving**. The world of YouTube Shorts is constantly evolving, and to stay on top, you need to be proactive about staying informed. Here are some next steps to continue your growth:

- **Join YouTube Creator Communities**: Whether it's Facebook groups, Reddit threads, or other forums, connecting with fellow creators can help you share insights, exchange strategies, and stay updated on the latest trends.
- **Analyze Top Creators**: Keep an eye on what the top creators in your niche are doing. Study their content, analyze their success, and see if there's anything you can apply to your own videos.
- **Continue Experimenting**: Never stop testing new ideas. Some of the best breakthroughs come from trying some-

thing unconventional. Don't be afraid to take risks with your content.

- **Use YouTube Analytics**: Dive deeper into YouTube's built-in analytics tools. These can give you invaluable insights into what your audience loves and how you can improve engagement.
- **Stay Consistent**: The best creators on YouTube didn't get there by posting once or twice. The secret to growth lies in **consistency**. Keep creating, learning, and refining your craft.

By following these next steps, you'll ensure that you don't just **create viral Shorts** once—you'll build a channel that thrives over the long haul. Keep your creativity flowing, stay adaptable, and **remember**: success on YouTube Shorts is a journey, not a destination. With persistence, dedication, and continuous improvement, you'll unlock the full potential of this powerful platform.

Your road to **YouTube Shorts success** starts now. Keep pushing forward, and watch your content—and your audience—grow like never before.